George and Smokey
A Tale of Two Cats

John Mitchell

Illustrated by Paul Crosley

authorHOUSE®

*All best wishes
John Mitchell
February 2016*

AuthorHouse™ LLC
1663 Liberty Drive
Bloomington, IN 47403
www.authorhouse.com
Phone: 1-800-839-8640

Published by AuthorHouse   08/06/2014

ISBN: 978-1-4969-3149-8 (sc)
ISBN: 978-1-4969-3148-1 (e)

In memory of my brother James J. Mitchell.

Thanks to my neighbor Bill Cox for the story.

This book is dedicated to my grandchildren,
Bryan, Emma, Layla and Jackson,
to my wife Leslie, and my family.

George and his brother Smokey lived outside Bill's home. Smokey was a grey shorthair cat, and his brother was a black and white shorthair. They hunted for mice and gophers in Bill's back yard.

Sometimes they went over the fence in the back yard and hunted in the woods behind Bill's house.

They made Bill happy because they caught mice and moles, and kept the rodents from eating the vegetables he grew in his garden.

John Mitchell

One day, George and Smokey had gone hunting past the fence and into the woods. Smokey knew that mice liked to live in brush piles, so he found a hiding place under a pile of limbs, and waited patiently for a mouse to show up.

Meanwhile, Bill went out into the backyard to mow his lawn.

Bill picked up a roll of chicken wire fence and tossed it on top of a pile of brush near the woods. He did not know that Smokey was hiding in the same brush pile. Smokey was startled, but he did not leave his hiding place because he was sure a mouse would come by any minute. He could smell them.

John Mitchell

After a while, Smokey got tired of waiting for mice. Bill had finished mowing his lawn and gone back into the house. Smokey was hungry and wanted to eat dinner on the porch with his brother. He began to climb out of the brush pile, but something was wrong. The hole he had entered was now blocked with the chicken wire.

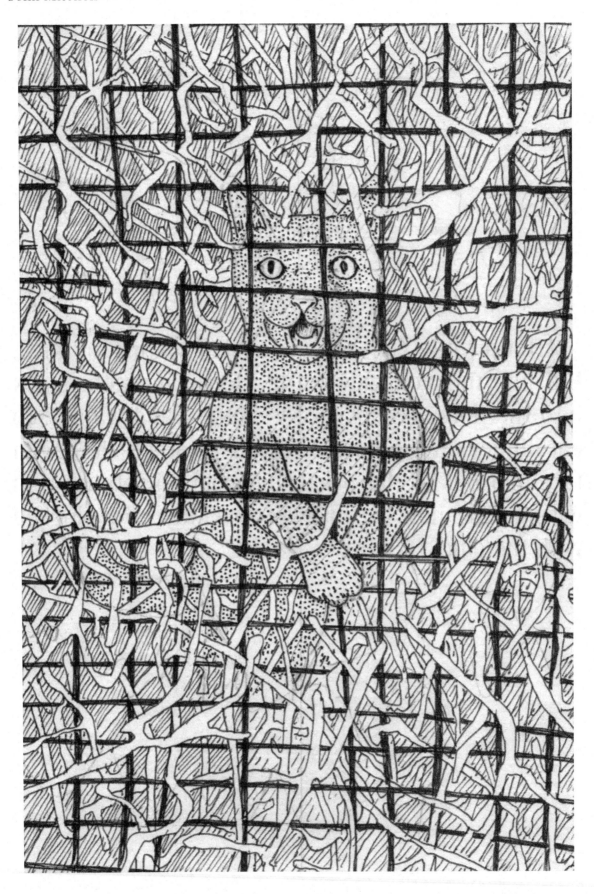

Smokey was a clever cat. He knew there should be another way out from under the brush, so he started to look. He crawled to his left, then his right, then he backed up, but he could not find another way to escape. There was no other way out. He was trapped!

Smokey let out a loud meow, hoping that Bill would hear him and move the wire fence, but Bill wasn't outside anymore. Smokey cried out again, and again. No one heard him. Smokey was in trouble!

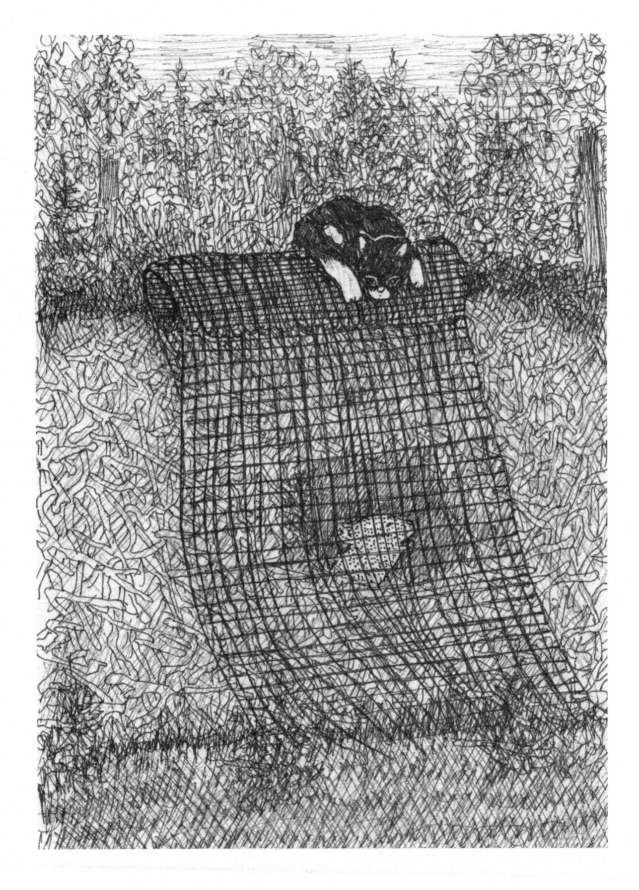

Pretty soon he heard George. He had come looking for Smokey. George climbed up on top of the chicken wire so he could see Smokey. He crawled down and around on both sides of the wire, but he could not find a way in to get to his brother.

The next morning, when Bill came out to feed the cats, George was there, but Smokey was missing. "That's odd," said Bill. "Where is Smokey? George, what did you do with your pal?'

As if to answer him, George headed toward the fence in the backyard, meowing as he went. But Bill wasn't watching; he was headed back inside the house.

The next morning Bill again noticed that Smokey was missing, but he figured that silly cat was visiting the neighbors, or was out in the woods hunting.

After several days and no sign of Smokey, Bill began to worry.

"I wonder what happened to my grey cat. I hope he hasn't run off, or gotten hit by a car." Bill searched everywhere he knew to look, but saw no sign of him.

Two weeks passed, and Bill had given up hope. Smokey was gone. Then one morning George ran up to Bill, stuck some claws in his leg, and yowled loudly.

"What's the matter, boy? What are you trying to tell me?" asked Bill.

Again George began to run toward the fence, as he had done several times before. This time Bill followed him. George slowed down so Bill could catch up. He jumped over the fence and ran to the brush pile. Bill walked through the gate and came over to him.

"George, what are you trying to show me?" Bill asked. "Do you know where Smokey is? Here, kitty, kitty!"

Bill heard a faint meow coming from one end of the brush pile. He walked over and picked up the roll of wire fencing. A grey streak shot out from under it, through the fence, and up to the house. Smokey had been freed at last! Bill looked around, and saw the remains of several mice and sparrows laying where Smokey had been captive. Bill looked at George in amazement.

"Well, I'll be! George, have you been bringing him food? He couldn't catch birds if he was trapped under here!"

Except for a momma kitty bringing food to her kittens, Bill had never heard of a cat doing this before.

George just meowed, sat down, and began to wash his front paw. His job was done and his brother was free. He stood and ambled toward the house, where Smokey was shoulder deep in the cat food, grumbling about his adventure between bites.

After Smokey finished eating and drinking some water, Bill picked him up to look him over. He had lost weight, but seemed to be fine otherwise. Bill scratched his chin and ears. Smokey purred louder than Bill could ever remember. He was happy to be free.

"That George is one fine cat," Bill said to Smokey. "He must love his brother very much to take care of you like he did. Someday I may have to take care of my brother like that."

John Mitchell

George just lay in the sun, twitching an ear. He had done well, but now it was nap time.

John Mitchell

Author's note: this is a true story about my neighbor's cats.

About the Author

John R. Mitchell is a graduate of Purdue University and spent most of his years working in the metal fabrication industry as a purchasing manager before he retired. He was born in Wisconsin, but currently lives in La Porte, Indiana. He is an air force veteran, having served in Vietnam.

CPSIA information can be obtained
at www.ICGtesting.com
Printed in the USA
LVOW03s1419111115
462065LV00001B/2/P